CHRISTMAS IN
BETHLEHEM AND JERUSALEM

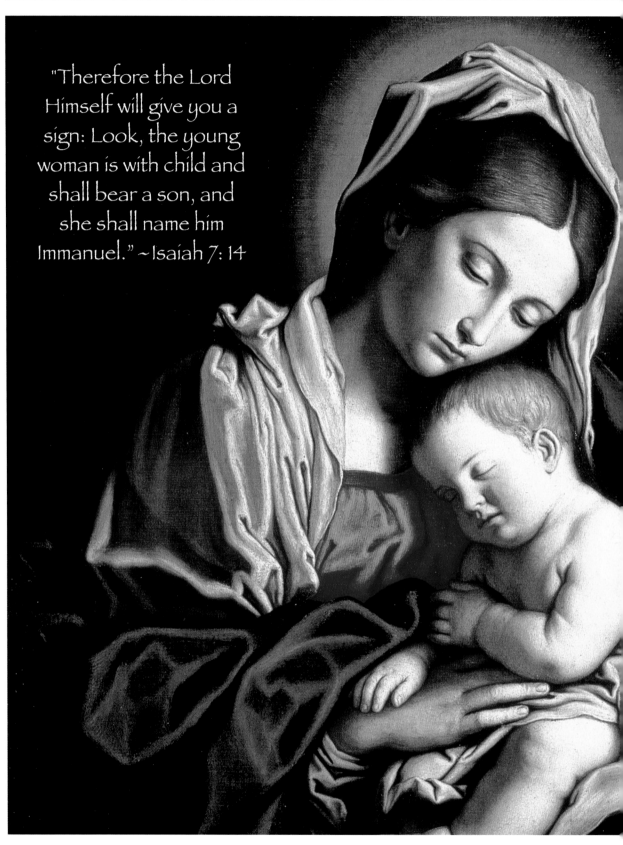

"Therefore the Lord Himself will give you a sign: Look, the young woman is with child and shall bear a son, and she shall name him Immanuel." ~Isaiah 7: 14

Madonna and Child: Giovanni Battista Salvi da Sassoferrato (1609-1685)

CHRISTMAS IN BETHLEHEM AND JERUSALEM

CHRISTMAS AROUND THE WORLD
FROM WORLD BOOK

WORLD BOOK, INC.

A SCOTT FETZER COMPANY

CHICAGO

STAFF

EXECUTIVE COMMITTEE

President
Donald D. Keller

Vice President and Editor in Chief
Paul A. Kobasa

Vice President, Sales and Marketing
Sean Lockwood

Vice President, International
Richard Flower

Controller
Anthony Doyle

Director, Human Resources
Bev Ecker

EDITORIAL

Associate Director, Annuals and Topical Reference
Scott Thomas

Managing Editor, Annuals and Topical Reference
Barbara A. Mayes

Senior Editor
Christine Sullivan

Consulting Editor
Daniel O. Zeff

Administrative Assistant
Ethel Matthews

Manager, Contracts & Compliance (Rights & Permissions)
Loranne K. Shields

Administrative Assistant
Gwen Johnson

GRAPHICS AND DESIGN

Senior Manager
Tom Evans

Coordinator, Design Development and Production
Brenda B. Tropinski

Senior Designer
Isaiah Sheppard

Media Researcher
Jeff Heimsath

Manager, Cartographic Services
Wayne K. Pichler

Senior Cartographer
John M. Rejba

MANUFACTURING/PRODUCTION

Director
Carma Fazio

Manufacturing Manager
Barbara Podczerwinski

Production/Technology Manager
Anne Fritzinger

Proofreader
Nathalie Strassheim

MARKETING

Manager
Tamika Robinson

Director, Direct Marketing
Mark R. Willy

Marketing Analyst
Zofia Kulik

EDITORIAL ADMINISTRATION

Director, Systems and Projects
Tony Tills

Senior Manager, Publishing Operations
Timothy Falk

Library of Congress Cataloging-in-Publication Data

Christmas in Bethlehem and Jerusalem.
    pages cm. -- (Christmas around the world)
   Summary: "A Christmas tour of the cities of Nazareth, Bethlehem, and Jerusalem, combining biblical texts concerning those cities with modern sites found in them. Also includes crafts, recipes, and carols"-- Provided by publisher.
   ISBN 978-0-7166-0824-0
   1. Christmas--Jerusalem. 2. Christmas--West Bank--Bethlehem. 3. Bethlehem--Social life and customs. 4. Jerusalem--Social life and customs. I. World Book, Inc.
   GT4987.81.W48C57 2013
   394.2663095694'42--dc23
                         2013020097

World Book, Inc.
233 N. Michigan Ave.
Chicago, Illinois 60601

Printed in China by Shenzhen Donnelley Printing Co., Ltd., Guangdong Province
1st printing September 2013

Bible passages quoted in *Christmas in Bethlehem and Jerusalem* are from *The Holy Bible,* New Revised Standard Version.

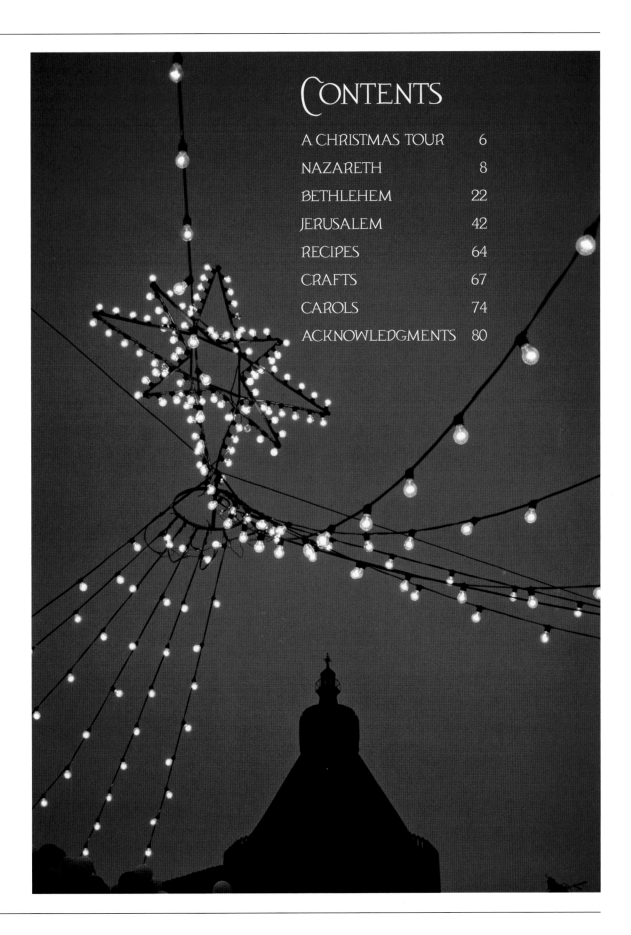

CONTENTS

A Christmas Tour

Our Christmas book is a tour of the cities that make up an important part of the Christmas story—Nazareth, Bethlehem, and Jerusalem. In this tour book, we combine the Biblical texts that tell the story of Christ's birth with the sites that you may see today in these three cities.

Our tour begins when our plane lands at Ben Gurion Airport, near the Israeli city of Tel Aviv. Tel Aviv is a modern city on the shore of the Mediterranean Sea. There are many ways to travel from Tel Aviv to other areas of the Holy Land. There are trains, taxis, and buses that run from the city to Jerusalem. Israelis drive on the right side of the road, as do Americans and Canadians, so renting a car and driving is familiar. Nevertheless, there are so many tour operators in this area of the world that it is probably easiest to book a guided tour of this region. A guided tour allows people familiar with the area to drive and navigate, and passing through checkpoints between

Israel and the West Bank becomes much easier. Often, churches and individual Christian denominations offer tours of the Holy Land at Christmas time. Taking such a tour allows visitors to be certain to visit the sites of greatest religious significance for them.

A bus ride from Ben Gurion to the first stop on our Christmas tour, Nazareth, takes around two hours.

Note: When visiting religious sites, it is a sign of respect for men and women to wear modest attire. Men should wear long pants, not shorts, and plain shirts. Women should wear long pants or skirts and long-sleeved shirts. Women may also need a head covering, such as a headscarf, at Muslim sites. At a synagogue or other place of religious observance for Jews, men may also be required to cover their head. One removes one's shoes to enter the interior of a mosque.

Nazareth

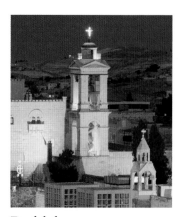

Bethlehem

Jerusalem

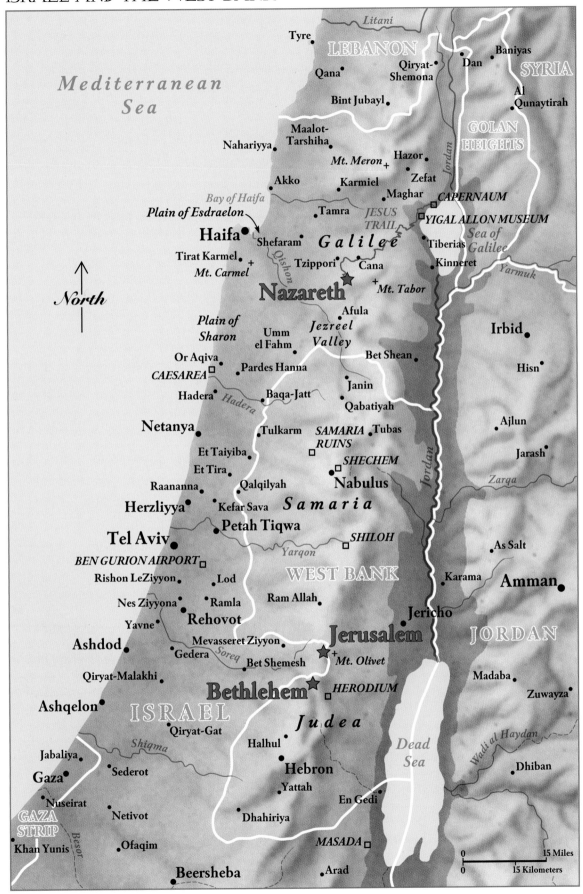

NAZARETH

The Christmas story begins in Nazareth. Nazareth is where the Annunciation took place—when an angel appeared to a maiden named Mary to tell her she would conceive a child of the Holy Spirit. It was in Nazareth that Joseph received a dream about the woman he was to marry. Nazareth was the home of Jesus for the time of his childhood until he began his ministry. And, so Nazareth begins our Christmas tour.

Nazareth is located between the Jezreel valley and the high hills of Galilee. The Jezreel valley is also known as the Plain of Megiddo. It was the site of many famous Old Testament battles—including the Battle of Megiddo, fought between the Egyptians and the Canaanites. So many biblical battles took place on this plain that the author of the Book of Revelation placed his predicted final battle between Good and Evil here. The word *Armageddon* is a Greek word taken from the Hebrew for Mount Megiddo.

Nazareth at the time of Christ was likely a small village in Galilee, a farming community. It had no importance at the time. There is no mention of Nazareth in the Old Testament or by such authors as the Jewish historian Josephus (who lived A.D. 37 to 100). Archaeologists can say, however, that Nazareth has been a continuous settlement since around 200 B.C. Archaeologists know that, by A.D. 66, Rome ruled Nazareth. In the A.D. 500's, the area came under the control of the Byzantine Empire. Nazareth was then taken over by the Crusaders—Christian warriors from Europe—in around 1000. The area was fought over by Muslims and Crusaders for the next two to three centuries. But, eventually, the Muslims won control. Under most Muslim rulers, Christians retained the right to control and worship in the holy places of Nazareth.

Over time, this small and unimportant town became a place of pilgrimage for Christians around the world.

"He will be called a Nazarene."
~Matthew 2:23

For a child has been born for us, a son given to us; authority rests upon his shoulders, and he is named Wonderful Counselor, Mighty God, Everlasting Father, Prince of Peace.

~Isaiah 9:6

In the sixth month the angel Gabriel was sent by God to a town in Galilee called Nazareth, to a virgin engaged to a man whose name was Joseph, of the house of David. The virgin's name was Mary. And he came to her and said, "Greetings, favored one! the Lord is with you."

But she was much perplexed by his words and pondered what sort of greeting this might be.

(continued on page 12)

The Prophet Isaiah, Sistine Chapel: Michelangelo (1475-1564)

The angel said to her, "Do not be afraid, Mary, for you have found favor with God. And now, you will conceive in your womb and bear a son, and you will name him Jesus.

He will be great, and will be called the Son of the Most High, and the Lord God will give to him the throne of his ancestor David.

He will reign over the house of Jacob forever, and of his kingdom there will be no end."

The Annunciation: Leonardo da Vinci (1452-1519)

Mary said to the angel, "How can this be, since I am a virgin?"

The angel said to her,

"The Holy Spirit will come upon you, and the power of the Most High will overshadow you; therefore the child to be born will be holy, he will be called Son of God."

~Luke 1:26-35

Now the birth of Jesus the Messiah took place in this way. When his mother Mary had been engaged to Joseph, but before they lived together, she was found to be with child from the Holy Spirit. Her husband Joseph, being a righteous man and unwilling to expose her to public disgrace, planned to dismiss her quietly. But just when he had resolved to do this, an angel of the Lord appeared to him in a dream and said, "Joseph, son of David, do not be afraid to take Mary as your wife, for the child conceived in her is from the Holy Spirit. She will bear a son, and you are to name him Jesus, for he will save his people from their sins."

~ Matthew 1:18-21

St. Joseph and the Christ Child: Guido Reni (1575-1642)

Sites of Nazareth

A number of important places in the Old City section of Nazareth are churches. Many of these churches are built over sites where tradition holds that an important event from the Christmas story occurred. Some of these sites have been chosen because of the Roman Emperor Constantine the Great (275-337). He was the first Roman Emperor to convert to Christianity, and he sent his mother, the Empress Helena, to the Holy Land in the 320's to discover relics of Christ and holy sites. Both the Church of the Nativity in Bethlehem and the Church of the Holy Sepulcher in Jerusalem are located on sites chosen by Helena.

The Roman Catholic Basilica of the Annunciation is near to the Church of St. Gabriel and is at the site where Roman Catholics believe the Annunciation occurred. Inside the church is the Grotto of the Annunciation, which many Christians believe to be the home of Mary. The current church was finished in 1969. However, in the lower areas of the church, remnants of an earlier church from the time of the Constantine and another from the time of the Crusades (1000) can be seen.

Mount Tabor stands alone about 6 miles (10 kilometers) east of Nazareth. Many Christians believe this was the site of the Transfiguration, when Christ appeared to his disciples physically changed and radiant. At the top of Mount Tabor is the Church of the Transfiguration, a Roman Catholic church built over the remains of a Byzantine and a Crusader church. The Franciscan monks maintain an associated monastery on Mount Tabor. There is also a Greek Orthodox church and monastery there.

One of the oldest attractions in Nazareth is the Church of St. Gabriel, also called the Church of the Annunciation. This Eastern Orthodox church was built over a stream. In Eastern Orthodox belief, Mary was drawing water at a stream when the angel Gabriel appeared to her. The first church on this site was likely built during the reign of the Emperor Constantine. Below the church there is a barrel-vaulted chapel, the Chapel of the Spring.

St. Joseph's Church is also in Nazareth's Old City. It is a Roman Catholic church rebuilt in 1914 on the site where tradition holds Joseph had his carpentry workshop.

A mosaic floor from an ancient synagogue in Tzippori, or Sepphoris, can be seen about 4 miles (6 kilometers) northwest of Nazareth. This small village is, in Christian tradition, the birthplace of Christ's mother Mary. It is now a national park that holds many archaeological treasures—including a Roman theater and a fortress built by Crusaders.

The White Mosque, built in the late 1700's and early 1800's by
Sheikh Abdullah al-Fahoum. After his death, he was buried in the
mosque's courtyard; his family still maintains the structure today.
The mosque is an important ecumenical force in Nazareth.

THE JESUS TRAIL

The countryside of Galilee is filled with sites from the New Testament. The Jesus Trail is a 40-mile (65-kilometer) walk from Nazareth to Capernaum. Some of the highlights of the walking tour include Cana, where the New Testament book of Mark places the miracle of Christ changing water to wine at a wedding; the Yigal Allon Museum, which houses a fishing boat from around A.D. 50, similar perhaps to the boat used by Christ and his disciples; and Capernaum, rich in archaeological remains. The walk can be completed in 4 to 5 days and requires no special equipment save comfortable shoes and sufficient water. Walkers should be fit enough to hike 10 miles (16 kilometers) in one day. There are a myriad of inns and guesthouses dotting the trail that offer accommodations to walkers. The trail is marked from Nazareth to Capernaum with orange and white blazes painted on boulders and the walls of buildings.

Ruins of a synagogue from the A.D. 300's, with the Sea of Galilee in the distance.

BETHLEHEM

Our next stop is Bethlehem, the birthplace of Christ. Because Bethlehem is so close to Jerusalem, we'll stay in at a hotel in Jerusalem and travel into Bethlehem. The trip from Nazareth to Jerusalem is about 90 miles (145 kilometers) and takes a little under 2 hours. The distance is 6 miles (9.6 kilometers) between Jerusalem and Bethlehem.

Bethlehem was a small village at the time of Christ's birth, but today it is a bustling town. For more than 1,000 years, the city has depended upon pilgrims and tourists for its livelihood. Many of the famous places in Bethlehem have an associated church at the site. This is especially true for the traditional place of Christ's birth, now surrounded by the Church of the Nativity.

Note: Bethlehem is in the West Bank and under the control of the Palestinian Authority. There is an Israeli military checkpoint on the road between Jerusalem and Bethlehem. You will not be checked going from Jerusalem into the West Bank, but you will need to show a passport and perhaps pass through a metal detector to get back into Jerusalem. Many organized tours include Bethlehem on their itinerary, but if you choose to tour on your own, buses run between Jerusalem and Bethlehem. You can also take a taxi from Jerusalem's Damascus Gate, get out and walk through the checkpoint, and catch a different taxi on the other side of the checkpoint into Bethlehem.

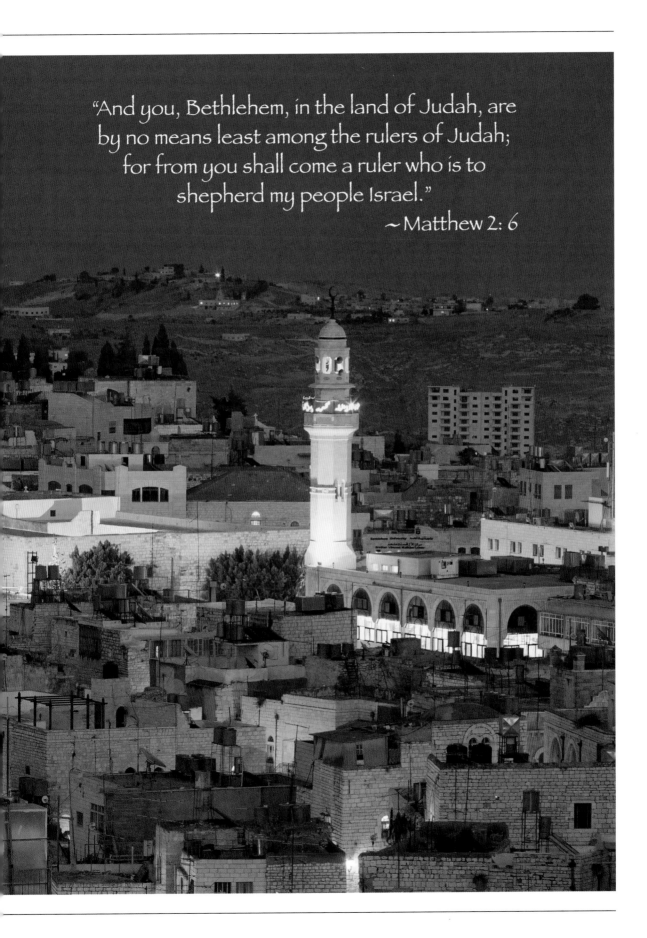

"And you, Bethlehem, in the land of Judah, are
by no means least among the rulers of Judah;
for from you shall come a ruler who is to
shepherd my people Israel."
~ Matthew 2: 6

In those days a decree went out from Emperor Augustus that all the world should be registered. This was the first registration and was taken while Quirnius was governor of Syria. All went to their own towns to be registered. Joseph also went from the town of Nazareth in Galilee to Judea, to the city of David called Bethlehem, because he was descended from the house and family of David. He went to be registered with Mary, to whom he was engaged and who was expecting a child.

~Luke 2:1-5

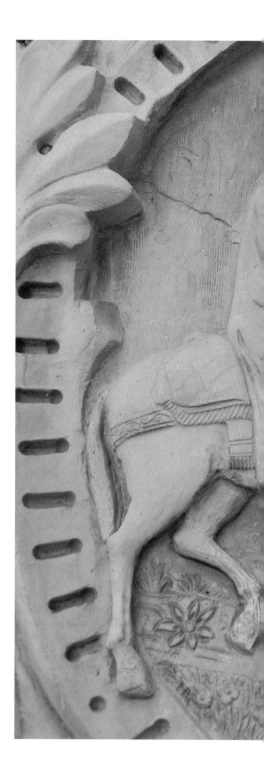

Bas relief of holy family at entrance to Bethlehem's Milk Grotto

While they were there, the time came for her to deliver her child. And she gave birth to her firstborn son and wrapped him in bands of cloth, and laid him in a manger, because there was no place for them in the inn.

~ Luke 2: 6-7

In that region there were shepherds living in the fields, keeping watch over their flock by night. Then an angel of the Lord stood before them, and the glory of the Lord shone around them, and they were terrified. But the angel said to them, "Do not be afraid; for see—I am bringing you good news of great joy for all the people: to you is born this day in the city of David a Savior, who is the Messiah, the Lord. This will be a sign for you: you will find a child wrapped in bands of cloth and lying in a manger."

(continued on page 28)

The Birth of Christ: Hans Leonard Schaufelein (1480-1540)

And suddenly, there was with the angel a multitude of the heavenly host, praising God and saying,

"Glory to God in the highest heaven, and on earth peace among those whom he favors!"

When the angels had left them and gone into heaven, the shepherds said to one another, "Let us go now to Bethlehem and see this thing that has taken place, which the Lord has made known to us." So they went with haste and found Mary and Joseph, and the child lying in the manger.

~Luke 2:8-16

A fresco from the church at Shepherds' Field, near Bethlehem.

In the time of King Herod, after Jesus was born in Bethlehem of Judea, wise men from the East came to Jerusalem, asking, "Where is the child who has been born king of the Jews? For we observed his star at its rising, and have come to pay him homage."

~Matthew 2:1-2

The Three Kings: Leopold Kupelwieser (1796-1862)

CHRISTMAS IN BETHLEHEM

Those words evoke images of a silent, reverent, alabaster city, waiting expectantly on a quiet and starry night. The realities of Christmas in modern-day Bethlehem are, however, very different. The endless conflict in the Middle East guarantees the presence of troops whenever and wherever crowds gather for major festivals. And the tendency of modern societies to make commercial capital on any event or place of importance is not absent in Bethlehem. The town's aggressive merchants loudly hawk their wares—even on Christmas Eve and Day.

Perhaps, most importantly, the Christians who come to Bethlehem to celebrate Christmas are no longer a unified group. Today, Eastern Christians, including Greek and Syrian Orthodox, Egyptian Coptics, and many others; and Western Christians, including Roman Catholics, Anglicans, and such Protestant groups as Lutherans; all have a claim on Bethlehem's Christmas. In fact, not all Christians celebrate Jesus' nativity on the same date.

As a result of Christianity's fragmentation, many shrines are held exclusively by one body; others are debated as to authenticity; and different groups maintain competing shrines. Many of the most important Christian holy places are in the hands of the Eastern Orthodox. This is the Christian church that received its legacy from the an-

cient church of the Eastern Roman Empire and then, later, from the successor state of the Byzantine Empire. Despite the fall of Constantinople and, with it, the Christian Empire of Byzantine Rome in 1453, the Eastern Orthodox Church has, down through the centuries, held on to many of its holy places. And so it is that the holiest place in Bethlehem, the Church of the Nativity—

On Christmas Eve, outside Bethlehem's Church of the Nativity, Roman Catholic clergy await the procession of the Latin Patriarch of Jerusalem. The church is believed to be the world's oldest Christian church in continuous operation. It was first completed in 339 by the Emperor Constantine. It was damaged and rebuilt by the Emperor Justinian in 565. It was extensively built upon and decorated by Crusaders in the 1000's and 1100's. The church is located over the spot traditionally held to be the birthplace of Christ.

traditional site of the birth of Jesus—is held by the Eastern Orthodox. To a lesser extent, the Roman Catholics, known as "Latin Christians" in the Middle East, hold important Christian sites in the Holy Land. These are largely the legacy of the Crusades of the Middle Ages, when Crusader armies of France, Germany, and other western Catholic lands conquered the Holy Land for pope and church.

WHEN IS CHRISTMAS?

In the United States and many areas of Europe, Christmas Eve and Christmas Day are celebrated on December 24 and 25, respectively. But, not everyone celebrates the birth of Christ on the same day. In the Eastern Churches, the date of celebration was January 6, or the Epiphany, when tradition holds that the Wise Men visited Christ. Armenian Orthodox Christians still celebrate on January 5 and 6 of the Western, or Gregorian calendar. Many other Eastern Orthodox Christians celebrate Christmas on December 25 of the Julian calendar, which translates to January 7 on the Western calendar. Most Orthodox Christians in the United States celebrate Christmas on December 25 of the Western calendar. Ethiopian Coptics also celebrate Christmas on that day.

Fireworks explode over a massive Christmas tree as children's choirs sing carols in Manger Square, in the heart of Bethlehem's Old City. The square is the focus of Christmas festivities in Bethlehem.

The Greek Orthodox patriarch of Jerusalem leads a Christmas Eve procession in Bethlehem. While the Roman Catholic Christmas Eve procession is held on December 24 by the Western calendar, the Greek Orthodox procession is on January 6.

The cloister of St. Jerome (347-420), outside the Church of the Nativity, allows access to a cave beneath the church where St. Jerome made his study and spent 30 years translating scriptures from Hebrew and Greek into Latin. This Latin translation of the Bible is known as the Vulgate.

The front door to the Church of the Nativity, the Door of Humility, is only 4 feet (1.2 meters) tall and 2 feet (.6 meter) wide. It requires visitors to bow down to pass through. The door was lowered in the time of the Ottomans to force riders on horseback to dismount before entering the church.

Wooden trapdoors in the nave of the church can be lifted to reveal geometrical mosaics on the floor, essentially all that remains of Emperor Constantine's original church.

The columns in the aisles and nave of the Church of the Nativity were painted by Crusader artists and depict images of saints.

A boy places a cross on the silver star in the grotto of the Church of the Nativity.

THE SILVER STAR

The silver star in the grotto of the Church of the Nativity was the cause, or at least was an excuse given as the cause, of the Crimean War (1853-1856). This war was fought by Russian forces against the allied armies of Britain, France, the Ottoman Empire (now Turkey), and Sardinia. The war's name comes from the Crimean Peninsula, an area of present-day Ukraine where much of the fighting took place. While the war was really about ports and shipping lanes, many of the issues most argued about centered on religious control of places in the Holy Land, which at that time were ruled by the Muslim Ottoman Empire. Decrees from that empire in the 1600's and 1700's had granted control of the churches and holy places to the Roman Catholic Church. However, the majority of practicing Christians in the Holy Land at this time were Eastern Orthodox Christians. The ruler of Russia, Czar Nicholas I (1796-1855), wanted to be seen as protecting the Orthodox faithful in the Holy Land. The ruler of France, Louis Napoleon (Napoleon III, 1808-1873) wanted to be seen as protecting Roman Catholic interests in the Holy Land. The French demanded that the Ottomans give up the keys to the main door to Church of the Nativity in Bethlehem and also requested the right to place a silver star at Christ's birthplace in that church. (A silver star at the site had been stolen in the 1840's. It was replaced by the sultan of Turkey, but the issue could not be resolved so easily.) France and Russia sent troops to the Holy Land. The United Kingdom and the Ottomans formed an alliance with France and also sent troops. Thus began one of the bloodiest wars of the 1800's.

The cave, or grotto, traditionally held to be Christ's birthplace has been venerated since A.D. 160. Several churches have been built over it since the church ordered by Constantine. The grotto, with the exception of the Altar of the Manger, is controlled by the Greek Orthodox, as is the church above it. (See page 62, "The Status Quo.")

The Roman Catholic patriarch of Jerusalem carries a statue of the Christ Child after midnight mass at St. Catherine's on Christmas Eve. This Roman Catholic Church adjoins the Church of the Nativity.

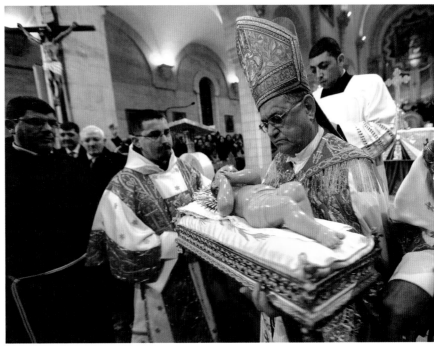

JERUSALEM

Our final stop on this Christmas tour is Jerusalem—a city considered holy by Christians, Jews, and Muslims. To walk in the Old City of Jerusalem is to enter an ancient world of the Bible in modern times. In the time of Jesus, Jerusalem was at the center of Jewish worship.

Jews in the time of Jesus lived a rich religious life. Every important event in the life of the individual and in the life of the family was accompanied by a rite that was religious, and often sacrificial, in character. The center of the religious life of all Jews was the great Temple. At times of high feasts and other important events, Jews journeyed to Jerusalem, to the Temple.

The Temple in the time of Jesus was the third structure that had been constructed on the Rock of Abraham—the site, by tradition, where Abraham had been prepared to sacrifice his son Isaac to the Lord. Jesus was taken to the Temple of Herod, which was begun around 20 B.C. by Herod the Great. (This structure, the last Jewish structure to be built over the Rock of Abraham, was leveled by the Romans in A.D. 70.)

"... and many nations shall come, and say: "Come, let us go up to the mountain of the Lord, to the house of the God of Jacob; that he may teach us of his ways and we may walk in his paths. For out of Zion shall go forth instruction, and the word of the Lord from Jerusalem."

~Micah 4:2

Christmas in Bethlehem and Jerusalem

The first Temple on this site was built by Solomon, son of David, and was destroyed by the invading armies of Nebuchadnezzar, King of Babylon. The innermost sanctum of the Temple of Solomon was called the "Holy of Holies" and contained the Ark of the Covenant, the cask that held the tablets upon which God had written His commandments to the chosen people.

The second Temple was hurriedly built at the end of the Babylonian exile and was far less elaborate than the Temple of Solomon. The Ark and the Tablets of the Lord had been lost. Herod pulled down the second Temple to make way for the third, which was, according to accounts, the most magnificent structure in the world. Even the Romans were awed by its walls of white marble and gold.

A Jewish family with a newborn first son was required to celebrate at least two religious rites shortly after the birth. The mother, considered ritually unclean for 40 days after childbirth, was to bring a lamb and a pigeon or dove to the priest in the Temple for sacrifice. A poor woman could omit the lamb and bring two birds. This Mary did.

A second rite celebrated the gift of a first-born male to the family and required the sacrifice of a beast, either a bull or a ram, as a sign of the child's redemption. Mary and Joseph had performed for Jesus the second rite, perhaps combined with the first. It is likely that pigeons or doves were substituted for the sacrificial beast.

Thus, an important ritual at the start of Christ's life took place in Jerusalem, at the temple. While most of the sites to be seen in Jerusalem relating to Christianity concern Christ's death there, the Western Wall, the last remnant of the temple, concerns a ritual practiced soon after the birth of Christ.

Presentation of Christ in the Temple: Andrea Mantegna (1431-1506)

When the time came for their purification according to the law of Moses, they brought him up to Jerusalem to present him to the Lord (as it is written in the law of the Lord, "Every firstborn male shall be designated as holy to the Lord"), and they offered a sacrifice according to what is stated in the law of the Lord, "a pair of turtledoves or two young pigeons."

Now there was a man in Jerusalem whose name was Simeon; this man was righteous and devout, looking forward to the consolation of Israel, and the Holy Spirit rested on him.

It had been revealed to him by the Holy Spirit that he would not see death before he had seen the Lord's Messiah. Guided by the Spirit, Simeon came into the temple, and when the parents brought in the child Jesus, to do for him what was customary under the law, Simeon took him in his arms and praised God, saying,

"Master, you are now dismissing your servant in peace, according to your word; for my eyes have seen your salvation, which you have prepared in the presence of all peoples, a light for revelation to the Gentiles and for glory to your people Israel."

~ Luke 2:22-32

The Western Wall, sometimes called the Wailing Wall, is all that is left of Herod's Temple today. This place is sacred in Judaism, as Jews believe that the place where the Temple once stood is holy. The Temple is believed to have been built on the site where Abraham prepared his son Isaac for sacrifice. This Temple was the place of Christ's presentation in Jerusalem.

Today, Jews congregate on the plaza in front of the wall to pray, but anyone is allowed to pray here. The prophet Isaiah refers to this place as "a house of prayer for all nations." People often write prayers on slips of paper, which they slip into the chinks between the stones of the wall.

Note: Men and women are segregated at the wall. Walk to the section of the wall appropriate to your gender. Long pants and sleeved shirts are appropriate for men and women. Men must cover their heads, a baseball cap will do, but yarmulkes are provided. Women, even married women, need not cover their head. There are washing stations at the wall so you may wash your hands before you pray.

The Western Wall is a retaining wall built to enclose the entire Temple Mount, the huge hill on which Solomon's Temple, and later, the Temple of Herod, were built. The Temple Mount is the third-most sacred site for Muslims, after Mecca and Medina. Muslims call the Temple Mount *al-Haram al-Sharif,* or the *Noble Sanctuary.* The golden Dome of the Rock covers the stone that Jews believe to be the holiest place on Earth and that Muslims believe to be the place where Muhammad ascended into heaven on his Night Journey. The Dome of the Rock may be seen from many locations in Jerusalem (see photograph on page 43). We cannot actually visit the Temple Mount on our tour, as it is closed to non-Muslims.

Markets abound in the narrow lanes of Jerusalem's Old City.

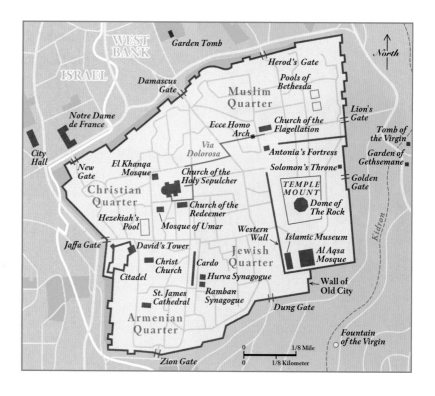

The Jaffa Gate is near the markets of the Old City, a must for us on our tour. Jerusalem's outdoor markets sell nearly any food item—oranges, nuts, spices, fish, pastries, sweets—in addition to clothing, fabric, and Judaica.

This is a book about Christmas, but no one touring the Holy Land would want to miss the sites Christ visited at the end of his life. The *Via Dolorosa* (or *Way of Grief,* in Latin) follows the traditional route that Christ took during his trial, execution, and burial. There are 14 stations on the *Via Dolorosa*—the first 9 appear on the streets of Jerusalem, the last 5 are inside the Church of the Holy Sepulcher (see pages 56-61). The Church of the Holy *Sepulcher* (that is, *Tomb*) is called the Church of the Resurrection *(Anastasis)* by Eastern Orthodox Christians.

All stations of the *Via Dolorosa* are identified with a plaque and many with a Roman numeral denoting which station it is. Some of the plaques are difficult to spot. It is preferable to take a guided tour of the way, and there are many guides available. On Fridays, the Franciscans walk the *Via Dolorosa* with pilgrims, which is a great way to walk the trail. Some of the events depicted in the stations are from biblical texts, but others depict events based upon tradition.

All stations of the *Via Dolorosa* are identified with a plaque.

The *Via Dolorosa* begins at Lion's Gate (left) in the Muslim Quarter of Jerusalem. The 1st station on the path represents Christ's trial and condemnation by Pontius Pilate. The location is actually inside a Muslim school, but visitors are often not permitted inside during school hours. Instead, go to the nearby Church of the Flagellation, operated by the Franciscans.

Within the same Franciscan compound is the 2nd station. at the Church of the Condemnation and Imposition of the Cross, which marks the place where Jesus took up the cross.

Also near to this station is the Ecce Homo Arch (right); *Ecce Homo* is Latin for *Behold the Man,* the words Pilate spoke when he presented Christ to the crowd after having him scourged and crowned with thorns.

The Catholic Polish Chapel marks the 3rd station, where Christ fell for the first time carrying the cross.

The 4th station marks the spot where popular tradition holds that Mary first saw Christ carrying his cross. The Armenian Church at this site is the Church of Our Lady of the Spasm. The Polish artist Zieliensky carved this bas-relief (above) on the church exterior.

The 5th station marks the place where Simon of Cyrene was ordered to carry the cross for Jesus for a time. In the wall of the chapel that marks this station is a stone that the faithful believe was touched by Christ. Pilgrims following the *Via Dolorosa* often touch or kiss the stone (right).

At the 6th station, a small brown door marks the place where Veronica is said to have wiped Christ's face with her veil—an imprint of his face is said to have been left on the veil. The name *Veronica* is a compound of the Latin words *vera icon*, which means *true image*.

Two Franciscan chapels mark the 7th station, where Christ again fell with the cross. The 8th station marks the place where Christ encountered the pious women. Christ tells the women that they should not weep for him, but for themselves and their children. The 9th station marks the final place where Christ fell with the cross.

For the last 5 stations—stations 10 through 14—we move inside the Church of the Holy Sepulcher, which is built on the site thought to be *Golgotha* (*place of the skull*, in Aramaic) or *Calvary* (in Latin), where Christ was executed and buried.

The church was originally built in the 300's by the Emperor Constantine. It has been damaged, destroyed, and rebuilt many times over. In the 1000's, the church was destroyed by the Fatimid Caliph al-Hakim. Crusaders rebuilt it in the 1100's. At that time, the Crusaders appointed three churches as guardians of the site: the Greek Orthodox, the Armenian Apostolic, and the Roman Catholic. In the 1800's, the Coptic Orthodox, the Ethiopian Orthodox, and the Syrian Orthodox gained smaller roles in responsibility for the church.

The denominations have not always been in harmony over the ensuing centuries. (See page 62, the Status Quo.) Much of the interior of the church is broken up into small chapels. Since differing denominations have various sensibilities as regards church decoration, the interior of the church is visually complex.

As you enter the Church of the Holy Sepulcher, you climb a steep flight of stairs; you are climbing the hill of Calvary. The Roman Catholic Chapel of the Franks forms the 10th station of the Via Dolorosa, marking where Jesus was stripped of his garments. The 11th station is the Roman Catholic Chapel of the Nailing to the Cross (left). A fresco depicting Christ being placed on the cross as Mary watches is at the 11th station. The mosaic on the ceiling of this chapel, showing the Ascension of Christ, is the only Crusader mosaic to have survived in the church.

The 12th station of the Via Dolorosa is the Greek Orthodox Chapel of the Crucifixion (right). It is Golgotha, the place where Christ died on the cross.

Station 13, inside the Rotunda of the church, is the Stone of *Unction (Anointing),* where believers meditate on Christ's body being prepared for burial. The outer walls of the Rotunda date back to Constantine's original church.

Station 14, the last station of the Via Dolorosa, is believed to be the tomb where Joseph of Arimathea laid Christ's body. Surrounding this tomb is a shrine called the *Aedicule* (meaning *little house*). Christians believe this to be one of the holiest places on Earth.

The large nave of the church is controlled by the Greek Orthodox and is called the Catholicon. The Catholicon features a large *iconostasis* (a painted partition separating the nave of a church from the sanctuary), which is flanked by the thrones of the patriarchs of Jerusalem and Antioch.

Ethiopian monks live in cells on the roof of the Church of the Holy Sepulcher.

THE STATUS QUO

A church that is shared and controlled by different denominations is not always peaceful or harmonious. So it has been with both the Church of the Nativity in Bethlehem and the Church of the Holy Sepulcher in Jerusalem. The ruler of the Ottoman Empire, Sultan Osman III, grew weary of the fighting between the denominations that surrounded these churches. In the mid-1700's, he issued an edict stating that whatever denomination held a certain holy place would continue to do so with no changes from that time forward. Any change in routine or ownership had to be agreed to by all the denominations that share a holy place. The original edict was solidified with another edict from an Ottoman ruler in 1852 that referred to this system as the "Status Quo."

The Status Quo has solved some problems and exacerbated others. Clergy of different denominations do occasionally still fight over perceived attempts to annex more space in a church. Cleaning a space or moving objects within a church can serve as a flashpoint for arguments. But, since the 1900's, serious bloodshed has been avoided. On the other hand, it can be difficult to fix problems within a church, since everyone's agreement is needed to begin any project. The roof of the Church of the Nativity in Bethlehem has leaked horribly for many years, endangering priceless frescoes and mosaics, but the project has been mired in disagreement between the denominations that hold that church—the Greek Orthodox Church, the Roman Catholic Franciscans, and the Armenian Orthodox.

A ladder stands in the same place it has stood for centuries. Under the Status Quo, moving objects can lead to serious disagreement.

The Garden of Gethsemane is the place where Jesus prayed before his betrayal by Judas and arrest. Some of the olive trees in this garden are nearly 1,000 years old.

Mount Olivet is a series of hills to the east of Old Jerusalem. Your view of the city of Jerusalem from this site is breathtaking. Jews have been buried on this site for thousands of years. In Jewish belief, when the dead are resurrected at the coming of the Messiah, those buried at Mount Olivet will be first. This is the end of our Christmas tour, for Mount Olivet is the place where tradition holds that Christ ascended into heaven.

CHRISTMAS RECIPES

MAAMOUL

These delicate little cookies are decorated by pressing the finished, filled pastries into a maamoul mold. If you cannot find a mold to leave a patterned impression in the dough, you can use the tines of a fork.

2 cups all-purpose flour
½ cup fine semolina flour
1 tsp. baking powder
½ tsp. vanilla extract
¼ cup vegetable oil
1 tbsp. sugar
3 drops orange-blossom water
12 tbsp. butter, room temperature
1 cup whole, pitted dates
4 tbsp. butter
1 cup coarsely ground walnuts
¼ cup sugar
2 tbsp. water
maamoul mold or fork
confectioner's sugar (optional)

1. Line a baking sheet with parchment paper. Preheat oven to 350 °F.

2. Combine first seven ingredients in a mixing bowl. Add 8 tablespoons of butter. Knead for about 5 minutes or until mixture holds together and forms a ball. (Add the remaining butter from the 12 tablespoons, 1 tablespoon at a time, if needed.) Set aside.

3. Combine the dates and the 4 tablespoons of butter in a food processor. Process until dates are finely chopped.

4. In a mixing bowl, combine the walnuts, sugar, and water. Mix well.

5. To make cookies, form a ball from a heaping tablespoon of dough. Cup one hand, place ball of dough in that hand, and make a deep indentation in the ball. Place a small amount of date mixture or walnut mixture in the indentation. Bring edges of dough together so that filling is completely covered. Press the ball into a maamoul mold. Remove cookie from mold by rapping sharply on edge of table. Place on baking sheet. Repeat with remaining dough.

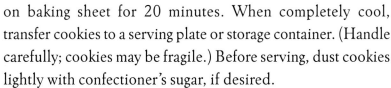

6. Bake for 20 minutes or until cookies are firm and the dough is slightly darker in color; do not allow to brown. Let cookies stand on baking sheet for 20 minutes. When completely cool, transfer cookies to a serving plate or storage container. (Handle carefully; cookies may be fragile.) Before serving, dust cookies lightly with confectioner's sugar, if desired.

Makes about 16 cookies

STUFFED DATES

24 pitted dates
24 whole almonds, blanched (without the skins)
1 cup semi-sweet baking chocolate, chopped, or semi-sweet chocolate chips
1 cup flaked coconut
1 skewer

1. Make a slit in each date and stuff it with an almond. This by itself is a delectable treat, but for a more elegant presentation, proceed to the next steps.

2. Line a baking sheet with parchment paper.

3. Melt chocolate in a microwave, checking often, and stirring to make sure chocolate does not burn. When chocolate is completely melted, pierce one date with a skewer. Dip date in chocolate. Rotate skewer so that excess chocolate falls off. Place date on parchment and sprinkle with coconut flakes. Repeat with remaining dates.

3. Refrigerate dates for 20-30 minutes or until chocolate has set.

Serves 6 (4 dates per serving)

CHRISTMAS CRAFTS

CHEERFUL ANGEL

1. Using wax paper, trace and cut out the patterns below to make a template.

2. Roll out enough clay to make a 4 in x 4 in (10 x 10 cm) sheet that is ⅛ in (0.3 cm) thick.

3. Position the templates on the clay and, with a knife or scissors, cut out one body and two arms.

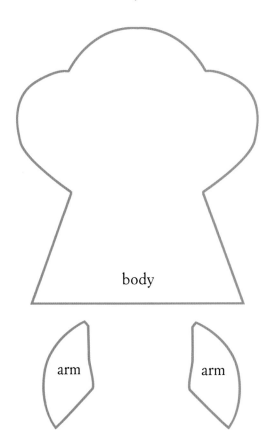

body

arm

arm

MATERIALS
- marker
- wax paper
- clay, see recipe on page 68
- rolling pin
- knife or scissors*
- cork from a bottle
- yarn
- tempera paint
- paintbrush

*ask an adult to help when using a knife

---

4. To make the head, press the clay around the cork as shown.

5. Turn the body over. Place a loop of yarn at the top and fill the cavity with a ball of clay that has one flat side. Press to seal.

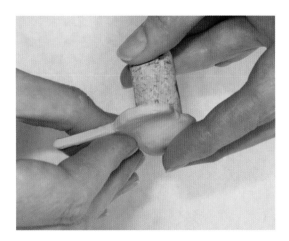

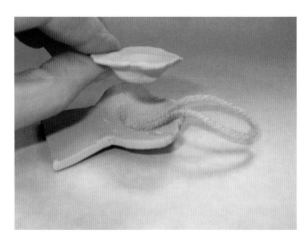

MODELING CLAY

1. Put on the apron, smock, or T-shirt to protect your clothes. Cover your workspace with newspaper.

2. Mix the flour, salt, water, oil, and cream of tartar in the saucepan.

3. Ask an adult to cook the mixture over low heat until thick. Then add food coloring until the dough is the color you want.

4. Let the dough cool. Then place it on a pastry board. Work the dough back and forth with your knuckles and palms.

5. Store the dough in a sealed plastic bag at room temperature.

MATERIALS
• apron, smock, or old T-shirt
• newspaper
• saucepan
• 1 cup flour
• ½ cup salt
• 1 cup water
• 1 tablespoon oil
• 1 teaspoon cream of tartar
• food coloring
• spoon
• pastry board
• plastic bag that seals

6. Attach the arms by first scoring the clay with a knife as shown. Press the arms in place.

7. Make two small balls for the hands and press into place.

8. Using the end of a paintbrush, draw lines into the wings. You can also draw lines into the bottom of the arms and the skirt.

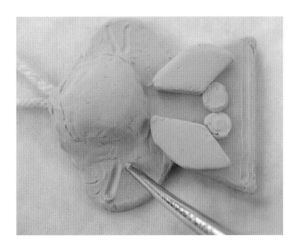

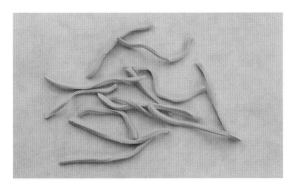

9. To make the hair, cut fine strips of clay and press around the head.

10. Allow the clay to dry.

11. Paint eyes, mouth, and dress decorations.

SILVER STARS

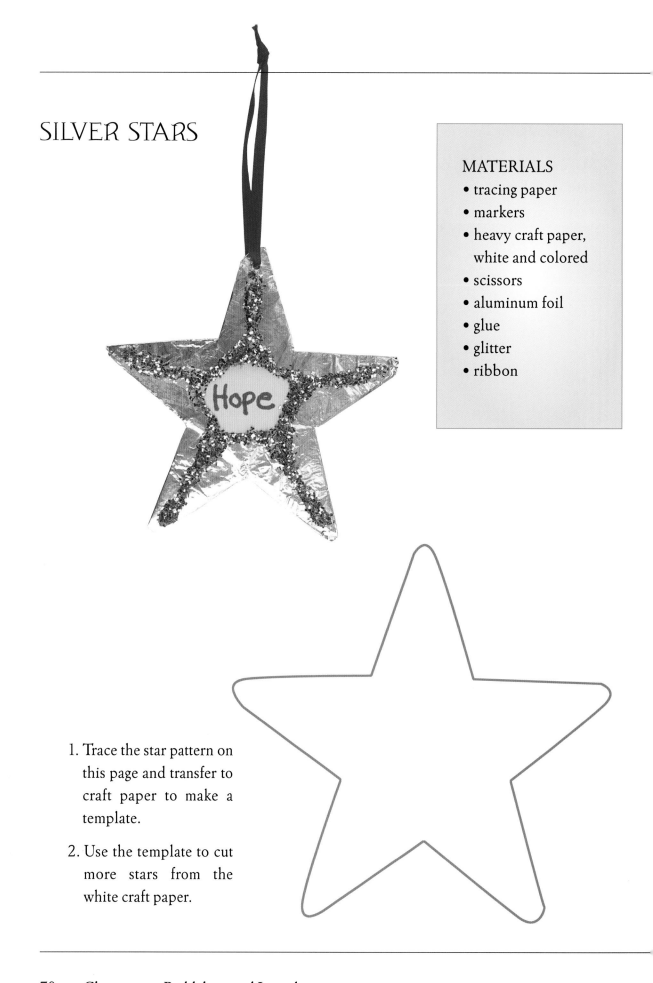

Hope

1. Trace the star pattern on this page and transfer to craft paper to make a template.

2. Use the template to cut more stars from the white craft paper.

3. To cover the stars, first cut a piece of aluminum foil twice as big as the star template. Fold the foil in half and cut out a star shape ¼ in (0.6 cm) larger than the template. Gently peel the two foil stars apart.

4. With the shiny side down, fold the foil edges over the paper star. Repeat this step to cover the other side.

5. Use colored craft paper and glitter to decorate the star as shown.

6. Poke a hole in the top point of the star and thread a ribbon through it. Knot the ribbon to make a hanger.

CHRISTMAS CAROLS

A mosaic of Christ in the Greek chapel (Catholicon) of the Church of the Holy Sepulcher in Jerusalem

AS WITH GLADNESS MEN OF OLD

William C. Dix, 1860

Arranged from Conrad Kocher, 1838

Moderato

1. As with gladness men of old Did the guiding star behold;
2. As with joyful steps they sped To that lowly manger bed,
3. As they offered gifts most rare, At that manger rude and bare,

As with joy they hailed its light, Leading onward, beaming bright;
There to bend the knee before Him whom heaven and earth adore;
So may we with holy joy, Pure and free from sin's alloy,

So, most gracious Lord, may we Evermore be led to Thee.
So may we with willing feet Ever seek Thy mercy seat.
All our costliest treasures bring, Christ, to Thee, our heav'nly King.

From *The International Book of Christmas Carols* edited by Walter Ehret
and George K. Evans. © 1963, 1980 by Walter Ehret and George K. Evans.
Reprinted by permission of Walton Music Corp.

O LITTLE TOWN OF BETHLEHEM

Phillips Brooks, 1868-1893

Louis H. Redner, 1868-1908 [WE]

Moderato

1. O lit-tle town of Beth-le-hem, How still we see thee lie! A-bove thy deep and dream-less sleep The si-lent stars go by; Yet in thy dark streets shin-eth The ev-er-last-ing Light; The hopes and fears of all the years, Are met in thee to-night.

2. For Christ is born of Ma-ry, And gath-ered all a-bove, While mor-tals sleep, the an-gels keep Their watch of won-d'ring love. O morn-ing stars to-geth-er Pro-claim the ho-ly birth, And prais-es-es sing to God the King, And peace to men on earth!

3. How si-lent-ly, how si-lent-ly The won-drous gift is given! So God im-parts to hu-man hearts The bless-ings of His heaven. No ear may hear His com-ing, But in this world of sin, Where meek souls will re-ceive Him still, The dear Christ en-ters in.

4. O ho-ly Child of Beth-le-hem! De-scend to us, we pray; Cast out our sin and en-ter in, Be born in us to-day. We hear the Christ-mas an-gels The great glad tid-ings tell; O come to us, a-bide with us, Our Lord In-man-u-el!

Bethlehem at dusk

A fresco of the Christmas story from the Church of the Nativity in Bethlehem

WHAT CHILD IS THIS?

William C. Dix, ca. 1865

17th Century English Air
Arrangement: John Stainer

Allegretto

1. What Child is this, __Who, laid to rest __ On Ma-ry's lap, __ is sleep-ing? Whom
2. Why lies He in __ such mean es-tate, __ Where ox and ass __ are feed-ing? Good
3. So bring Him in-cense, gold, and myrrh, Come peas-ant, King __ to own Him, The

an-gels greet__ with an-thems sweet, While shep-herds watch__are keep-ing?
Chris-tian, fear:__ for sin-ners here__The si-lent Word__is plead-ing?
King of kings, __ sal-va-tion brings, Let lov-ing hearts__en-throne Him.

REFRAIN

This, this __ is Christ the King;__Whom shep-herds guard and an-gels sing:
Nails, spear,__shall pierce Him through, The Cross be borne, for me, for you:
Raise, raise__ the song on high, __ The Vir-gin sings__her lull-a-by:

Haste, haste __ to bring Him laud,
Hail, hail, __ the Word made flesh, The Babe,__the Son__ of Ma-ry!
Joy, joy,__ for Christ is born,

From *The International Book of Christmas Carols* edited by Walter Ehret and George K. Evans. © 1963, 1980 by Walter Ehret and George K. Evans. Reprinted by permission of Walton Music Corp.

ACKNOWLEDGEMENTS

The publishers gratefully acknowledge the following sources for photography. Credits are listed from top to bottom and from left to right on their respective pages. All illustrations and maps were prepared by WORLD BOOK unless otherwise noted.

Cover: © Duby Tal, Albatross/Alamy Images
2:       *Madonna and Child* (c. 1600) oil on canvas by Sassoferrato, II, Palazzo Ducale (© Bridgeman Art Library)
5:       © Jon Arnold Images/Alamy Images
6:       © Reinhard Marscha, imagebroker/Alamy Images; © Stefano Baldini, Alamy Images; © Joachim Hiltmann/imag/imagebroker
8-9:   © Reinhard Marscha, imagebroker/Alamy Images
10:      *The Prophet Isaiah* (c. 1500) Fresco by Michelangelo Buonarroti, Sistine Chapel (© Bridgeman Art Library/Alamy Images)
12-13:   *The Annunciation* (c. 1470) Oil and Tempera on Panel by Leonardo da Vinci, Uffizi Gallery (© PAINTING/Alamy Images)
14:      *St. Joseph and the Christ Child,* (c. 1635) oil on canvas by Guido Reni, Museum of Fine Arts (© Bridgeman Art Library)
16:      © Shutterstock
17:      © Duby Tal, Albatross/Alamy Images; © Shutterstock
18:      © Shutterstock
19:      © Zev Radovan, BibleLandPictures/Alamy Images
20:      © PhotoStock-Israel/Alamy Images
21:      © Robert Harding World Imagery/Alamy Images
22-23:   © Stefano Baldini, Alamy Images
25:      © Imagebroker/Superstock
26:      *The Birth of Christ* (c. 1500) oil on panel by Hans Leonard Schaufelein, Hamburger Kunsthalle (© Bridgeman Art Library)
29:      © Shutterstock
30-31:   *The Three Magi* (1825) wood by Leopold Kupelwieser, Oesterreichische Galerie (© SuperStock)
33:      © Issam Rimawi, Zuma Press/Alamy Images
35:      © Abed Al Hashlamoun, EPA/Alamy Images; AP
36:      © Shutterstock; © Abed Al Hashlamoun, EPA/Alamy Images
37:      © Abed Al Hashlamoun, EPA/Alamy Images; © Shutterstock
38:      © Jim Hollander, EPA/Alamy Images
39:      © Oliver Weiken, EPA/Alamy Images; © Abed Al Hashlamoun, EPA/Alamy Images
40:      © MARKA/Alamy Images
41:      © Duby Tal, Albatross/Alamy Images
42-43:   © Joachim Hiltmann/imagebroker/SuperStock
44:      *Presentation of Christ in the Temple.* (c. 1465) Oil on poplar by Andrea Mantegna, Staatliche Museen (© Art Resource)
48:      © David Jennings, Alamy Images
50:      © Globuss Images/Alamy Images
51:      © Shay Levy, PhotoStock-Israel/Alamy Images
52:      © Ian Nellist, Alamy Images
53:      © Mark Daffey, Alamy Images
54:      © M. Sobreira, Alamy Images; © Shutterstock
55:      © Shutterstock
56:      © Zev Radovan, BibleLandPictures/Alamy Images
59:      © Tips Images/SuperStock
60:      © Sliman Khader, ZUMAPRESS/Alamy Images
61:      © Shutterstock; © Eliana Aponte, Reuters
62:      © Shutterstock
63:      © Matt Purciel, Alamy Images; © iStockphoto/Thinkstock
64:      © Karen Zack Ingebretsen
65:      © Karen Zack Ingebretsen; © Ali Hashisho, Reuters/Landov
66:      © Shutterstock; © Karen Zack Ingebretsen
67-73:   © Brenda Tropinski
74:      © Shutterstock
77:      © Stefano Baldini, Alamy Images
78:      © Vitalii Mykhailov, 123RF

Craft consultant:
Brenda Tropinski
Advent calendar:
Madonna and Child (c. 1600) oil on canvas by Sassoferrato, II, Palazzo Ducale (© Bridgeman Art Library)
Advent calendar and recipe card illustrations:
Eileen Mueller Neill
Recipe consultant and recipe card editor:
Karen Zack Ingebretsen